Scared Little Black Girl

by
Clintina Carmichael

Bloomington, IN Milton Keynes, UK

AuthorHouse™
1663 Liberty Drive, Suite 200
Bloomington, IN 47403
www.authorhouse.com
Phone: 1-800-839-8640

AuthorHouse™ UK Ltd.
500 Avebury Boulevard
Central Milton Keynes, MK9 2BE
www.authorhouse.co.uk
Phone: 08001974150

© *2006 Clintina Carmichael. All rights reserved.*

No part of this book may be reproduced, stored in a retrieval system, or transmitted by any means without the written permission of the author.

First published by AuthorHouse 10/26/2006

ISBN: 1-4259-7450-3 (sc)

Library of Congress Control Number: 2006909456

Printed in the United States of America
Bloomington, Indiana

This book is printed on acid-free paper.

In loving memory of Tyrone Johnson

For attaining wisdom and discipline; for understanding words of insight; for acquiring a disciplined and prudent life, doing what is right and just and fair; for giving prudence to the simple, knowledge and discretion to the young. Let the wise listen and add to their learning, and let the discerning get guidance.

Proverbs 1:2-5

Scared Little Black Girl

Life seems to be somewhat of a mystery. There are days that we feel we have a complete understanding of what we are to do. Then there are other days when we wake up and don't have a clue. It is likely the case that something will not go our way and we may start to feel upset or discouraged about something that we think should have happened. It is common to feel that when something goes our way we are thrilled. At that one moment in our lives, we seem to feel that we have accomplished some great goal.

I'm not sure if we ever stop to think how, when, and why things happen the way they do. Some people like to say that it's God; others say that it's luck. Some people say that Satan makes them do bad things. I believe that in one way or another, things are predestined: a conversation, a greeting, a new job, losing a job, or even meeting our mate. The bottom line is that we all have choices to make daily, including our courses of action.

As children, we look at television and start to imagine the things that we will do as we become young women or men. We understand that we're supposed to go to school, get an education, get married and have children, buy a house, and live happily ever after. Television even shows us that if we don't live the "American dream" that we can make it with children and with no husband. One thing that television doesn't show is how it all starts-- the pain of entering a bad relationship, the outcome of your choices. Television doesn't show us the determining factor of why some of us become successful and live that so-called American dream, while others have bad and then worse relationships that lead to having kids by three different men or women, and why some of us decided just to be single because it's not worth the potential pain or heartbreak. In many cases, we don't take the time to look at situations for what they are. Instead, we are distracted by the glamour or good things that we hope will come from a relationship, life, and attainable goals, which can determine if we have that American dream, or if we become another government study.

Many people are so caught up in this storybook life that they ruin themselves before they have a chance to succeed. I wanted that America dream, to have a husband that would rescue me from the wicked ways of the world and make all my dreams come true. So, I spent most, if not all my time attempting to figure out how I was going to get that right person, and would fantasize about the way my life should be. Most, if not all of us do this from time to time. We are caught in a world that is driven by the material things in life. The material things have become the center of our world. We spend much of our time daydreaming about the things that we should have done or the people that we should have become.

We do not realize that we must exercise sound judgment in practical matters and be very cautious in conduct. We have the freedom to make decisions and have good judgment. We should make it our goal to teach each other the errors of our ways, and to make sure that young and old people learn from our mistakes.

Scared Little Black Girl

As children, we don't understand the changes that will take place over the next seventy to ninety years. Our peers, parents, and family sometimes warn us of things that will, could, and may possibly happen to us as we mature from children to adults. There are some things that we retain and other information that is lost.

There was a time in my life that I established a plan for myself. I had this impeccable picture that I would grow up to be the picture-perfect person, who had a handsome man on a white horse, who would come and sweep me off my feet. Some time later, that same man would recite sweet words of his love and dedication to me in front of the ones that I held close to my heart. We would be deeply in love and have two children, a boy and girl, with a dog named Skip.

Now at the age of twenty-eight, life has shown me the difference in the choices that I make. There have been certain events that have happened in my life. There are some I can remember, ones that often bring a smile to my face, and others are somewhat hard to remember at all. It may seem strange that I'm stating that I can remember the bad events better than the good. I believe that our memories are a direct reflection of the choices that we make and serve as constant reminders of the paths that we should have taken daily. As a result, our minds linger on the memory of the repercussions of our decisions, based on our present circumstances. It's important that we get this information, for we should not be consumed by the realty of the world, for the world should not consume us.

It was once told to me to be careful of those I surround myself with. I always wondered why my grandmother and other family members would sit down and tell us story after story about how they grew up. It always seemed that the stories were warnings or dormant lessons waiting for me and my younger cousins to live and learn. At the time the stories were being told, we had no sense that those things could ever happen to us. In fact, I remember saying to myself that I will choose another step and that the end result will not be the same as my grandparents', aunts' or uncle's.

"Do you know?" This is the question that lingers in my mind. I assumed that things would always be as I perceived them to be. My family was not broken. I had a mother, a father, and a sister who was loving, when she wanted to be. There were the occasional arguments in my household. My mother and father would get upset with each other, like any other couple. They would disagree with a decision that the other partner made; but regardless of the arguments that took place, my father and mother always loved each other and made it work.

As a child looking at my father and mother, my personal relationship skills were developing and I wasn't aware of it. I don't think that my mother and father knew the kind of attention that I was giving their relationship, putting together the pieces, year by year, of how a woman and a man should treat each other. You see, we have to understand that children are like liquids and solids. We start in the liquid state and as we grow, we become solid. We are solid with all the things that happen, as we're growing up. The fun and sad times; the abuse mentally, physically and emotionally from our parents, grandparents, siblings, and people that have surround us our entire lives all plays a big part in molding us to become who we are. From the conversation and handling of situations, we learn how to respond appropriately. This gives us a sense of who we are, and whether we hold the value of ourselves and look at other individuals as important entities in this society.

Let's go back and try to remember when your mother or father was in a relationship with each other or another person, Think about some of the relationships that happened in the past and direct the attention to how the situation was handled. Was it somewhat similar to how you responded to that person? It often comes back to the fact that we're products of our environments. It takes a special person to not let the negative environment influence him or her. These are the people in the family that change the cycle that has been in place for years.

Let me give an example:

A person lives in a household with a working mother and no father. The mother is dating and bringing different men into the household.

The child can grow up to mimic her mother by working and thinking that it is okay to sleep with different men anytime she feels like it. The woman that overcomes this scenario will understand that her mother didn't value her body and proceeds to move in a different direction, other than sacrificing her own self-pleasure.

The problem with most of us is that we want to make a change and take a chance, but there is a hold on us because of this environment brainwashing. What is brainwashing? Brainwashing is defined as the application of a concentrated means of persuasion in order to develop a specific belief or motivation. This, in turn, translates into your inability to achieve a certain goal because of your circumstance. In all the products of your environment is a form of the slavery mentality that the worth of you is within your parents and the common trend of your family tree. You are who you are because of what you were introduced to; however, I'm a firm believer in taking what you have learned, sorting it out, choosing what you want to keep, and getting rid of the rest.

High School

Entering into high school, I had never been kissed by a boy. In fact, my menstrual cycle had not even arrived. On my first day of school, I noticed that there was something different about me than the other girls. I took a look around and saw that some were wearing make-up and others had different haircuts. It was strange to me that they were able walk out the house with little to no clothing on and all that stuff on their faces. I then began to look at the young boys that were standing around. Some of them were hanging out talking; others were checking out the girls, and some just had something else they wanted to do. I thought to myself, my mother never told me that people were going to look at me differently and form an opinion because of the way I dressed or talked.

As I continued my first day in school, no one spoke to me. In fact, it seemed as if everyone was staring at me because I was different. I thought that I had a different outlook on how things should be. My family didn't have much money, and so, I did not have the latest shoes or the fancy wardrobe. In reality, I had only one new outfit and the rest were old clothes that I matched together to look as if they were new. The emotions were raging inside of me, and I made a choice that there were only three ways that I could go.

I could be depressed, which is a form of sadness and discouragement; or I could have become embarrassed, which would have made me become self-conscious; or I may have become reluctant because of feeling ashamed.

Instead, none of these words came to mind. I decided at that moment to be confident in all of the decisions that I would make from that moment forward. So, I gathered my books and headed to my first class. I knew there were going to be obstacles and people who were going to test my level of confidence. We all need to understand that in this world, there is always someone smarter, thinner, stronger, and able to do things better than us. We can look at this as having a choice to be either weak or strong in mind. Ask yourself, "Am I a weak or strong-minded person?" If the choice is weak or strong, it does not make us more or less than someone else. This terminology isn't complicated. In each one of us, there are keys that will unlock secrets to our lives and that will reveal what the future holds. We will encounter different challenges in our lives by coming in contact with individuals that have different perceptions. They can also be described as unsympathetic or indifferent, in which cases, I called them estranged personalities. By evaluating the task and information we receive from our situation and life experience, one way or another, we will determine the path that lies ahead.

Emotional Roller Coaster

It has always been my experience that women and men think, feel, and accept issues, relationships, and everyday communication in various ways. I'm no expert on the topic of man versus woman, but I can say that women tend to be more emotional than men. By nature, it is our make-up to have a desire to be with one person that will love and value our needs in all aspects. In many cases, this is something that does not happen with most women, and we seem to leap from man to man in order to confront this emotional craving.

It is my observation that men deal with their emotions with a stonewall and stoic face. Men take on a relationship and don't understand the emotional distraught, which they may cause. Men think with their minds in reference to the heart. They understand that emotions are not going to solve the issues, but in contrast, create them. Let's compare a man to a paper bag.

This paper bag has numerous unique qualities. This bag can bend, fold, and be stepped on, and all the while, it still has the same form, color, and purpose to hold and place items in. A man is much like this paper bag; they are able to adjust and detach themselves from situations. They are able to go back to the original form after a bad, good, or disastrous circumstance. I am not saying that men don't have emotions. This is not a psychodynamic examination; while women can disregard emotional attachment the same as a man, it has been my understanding that the emotional strain is that much greater and more impinged. The attitude of not engaging in another relationship or disconnecting self from the social community can be that much greater from a woman versus a man. In turn, withdrawal of opposite sex conversation, connection, and opinions of what will be expected to happen start to come to mind when women detach emotional feeling.

I Think I'm In Love

During my freshman year in high school, more people were warming up to me and I began to have some close friends. Although still not the best dressed person in school, I knew what was wrong from right. I carried this with me and understood what I wanted to achieve. I started to notice some attention from quite a few guys. Some of the attention was from guys trying to figure me out and test the waters to find out what my reaction may have been if they approached me. The guys that had a sense of confidence about themselves and knew they would have a challenge getting me to do what they wanted to do seemed to be the ones that were most attracted to me. Walking down the hallway, I would turn and always look at a creation of pure beauty--a creature that was created for people to watch and admire, but I don't think that it was for touch. Almost like a movie, my days went in slow motion when I saw him. He was fine, with a sloppy hairdo and baggy pants. Most of the girls in high school liked him and wanted him to like them as well. One day while riding the bus on the way home, I glanced outside my small bus window and noticed him looking at me. A couple of days later, he approached me, asking for my phone number. I didn't know if he was approaching me because of the way I looked or because he wanted to talk to my sister. Surprised, I gasped for air and told him that I was not allowed to give my number out to boys. I felt my face become red and I could feel the heat coming off my face. I turned away for a moment, as I got my books out of the locker, as I calmed down and took a deep breath. I told him that I would have to ask my mother first before I gave my number out. He said cool and walked away like he had heard that line many times before. With anticipation, I road the bus and watched as he walked across the field, and daydreamed about how it would feel to talk with him on the phone or hold hands while walking in the hallway. I ran home and wrestled my sister and cousin for the phone to make a call to my mom. I told her what happened and that a boy wanted my phone number. I described him as a friend and simply let my mother know that he would call me only for small conversation. The phone went silent for a moment, and a sweet answer came from my mother, saying yes to me giving him the number. There were a few restrictions that I had to obey; I agreed and was able to give him my number. I was anxious to get to school the next day. I asked my sister to do my hair, and I ironed my clothes in preparation to see him again. That night, I couldn't sleep with all the ideas I had floating in my mind. I knew that I had to look my best.

Morning came, and I was the first dressed and ready to walk to the bus stop. I didn't have much to say that morning; I just wanted to get to school. The bus pulled up, and with excitement, I looked to the left and right of me as I was getting off the bus, hoping to see him walking across the field or hanging out in front of the school. First and second period went by and I had no sight of him yet. By the end of the day, I thought that I would not see him, until I walked to my locker to pack my bags. I heard a voice come from behind me and say, "Hey, are you allowed to give me your number?" I turned and said yes, and pulled the balled-up piece of paper from my pocket. With sweaty palms and nervous hands, I pulled it from a ball and straightened it out. I told him that my mom said that I could not receive calls after 9:00 p.m. He agreed that he would call me when he got home.

As I walked to the bus, I smiled and couldn't wait until the bus dropped me off. I kept conversation short with my friends and rushed home, did my homework, cleaned my room, and was ready and waiting for him to call. Finally, while I was waiting patiently by the phone, he called. It seemed that we were talking on the phone for the whole night, about nothing, of course, but for us it was a serious conversation. It was not my intention to have this guy as my boyfriend, because I was not allowed to have one. As time progressed in our friendship, it turned into a relationship.

We started to meet at the locker everyday, and he would carry my books to class. It felt like we were meant for one another. Our conversations started to get more intense, and his eyes drew me closer to his heart. Some time had passed and I knew that I was not what he was used to; I stuck to my guns and maintained the person that I was, never jeopardizing my self-worth. As we grew closer, it was bound to happen; I soon shared my first kiss with him: lip to lip and tongue to tongue. I had never experienced that feeling before. "Could this be love, or was he after something else that I was not ready to give?" The more time we spent together, I began to focus on him and he became the reason why I wanted to go to school, do my hair, and make sure that my clothes were neat and clean. I knew without a doubt in my mind that I was in love. One day, he told me the words that I was waiting to hear: "I love you." My heart stopped; the smile on my face said a thousand words. I'm certain of it. I said that I loved him, too, but did I know what love was? Was I just repeating what I had heard other people say?

The more and more we spent time kissing and holding one another, the more emotional lust developed in him and temptation stepped in. "No to sexual interaction," I said, and although he respected that in me, his experience before he met me would drive him to the next level of self satisfaction. There was no question in his mind about where I stood on the issue of sexual intercourse. You see, when I first met him, I remembered something that my sister told me at the beginning of my freshman year. My sister said that I needed to make sure that every boy that I had a conversation with knew that I didn't believe in premarital sex. This, she said, would set me apart from the other girls and I would find out who was interested in me and who simply wanted to have sexual interaction.

I told my boyfriend this and he was cool with it. What I didn't know at that time is that people often have a plan designed for us and we aren't aware of it. We know how to use certain words or even make someone feel obligated to us, when indeed we don't owe anyone anything at all. I knew for a fact that he loved me, because he respected the things that I was saying to him, but that made no guarantees that he would try to go after what he wanted; and that's he did. He caressed my mind and told me all the things that a young woman would want to hear, playing with my mind and taking my lack of knowledge of relationships to a different level. He would frequently use the words I love you, or I can't be without you. I took those words to heart and never let any other being interrupt what we had. I didn't listen to anyone about the rumors of him being a person that had many women, I didn't listen to the way that he talked to other girls or looked at the image that was portrayed in school.

His image became a direct reflection of who I was; the comparison of the company that you keep came into existence for me and I was labeled as being just like him. Although my value system was so different, we started to merge.

Time progressed, and I started to identify the things in him that were not pleasing to me or my heart. I began to analyze his look, walk, and talk, and I knew that something was not right about his feel. I was on a mission: a mission to save him. I felt that it was my responsibility to save him from the destruction that he was headed toward. I knew in my heart that if I gave all of my heart and gave all of myself to him that I would be able to change him and make him this great person. At the age of fifteen, it became my goal to help in every situation and confront him, to make sure that he was making the right choices. I started to try to understand how and when to object and react to his every emotion and body gesture. Did I set out to do this? Does this sound a little psychotic? Perhaps it does. I wanted to save someone from destruction; but truthfully, we all do it in one way or another. The pattern that I created was going to be my downfall in life. Many young and old people think we have the power to change someone with conversation and other qualities. We dictate to someone how they should live and react to situations. How many times have you suggested that your mate dress a certain way or talk to someone else in your presence in a certain fashion? I call this the saving and changing process.

> To save is to rescue or preserve from harm or danger, to preserve for future use, to prevent loss or waste. To change means to exchange, to make different, alter a substation, an altercation, or variation.

It is my belief that each of us, male or female, has a direct reaction to someone that has been seeking help and is trying to uplift himself by trying to make his life better. Our reason may be so that we can say that we had a role in making him or her a success, or so that the credit for this person being better than what he has historically been is credited to us. We walk in life, some big hero, demanding that it is better our way, devoid of thought about the life once encountered by trying to make him live against the odds of survival of past family riches and failures. Who said our way was the right way? Who said that we knew all the answers? Who said that we were going to be the ones that would set anyone free?

I have learned in my life that I cannot change or save people that are not willing to listen and understand their own lives. We have to understand that people only change to try to benefit someone else's lifestyle. In fact, I concluded that the more I impressed my ideas and lifestyle on him, he started to try to adapt, but he retaliated against me and my perfect plan.

More and more, I took time to understand what he was doing and to recommend things that he should do. I started to lose track of myself and the things that I should have been doing. I thought we were so close and we had each other to depend on. School came to an end and, although excited about the summer, I knew that I wouldn't see him everyday. That destroyed me because I knew that I would lose control. I was completely in love and willing to compromise myself to make sure that we had a connection that no one could break. I never stopped to think if he was ever feeling the same way about me. In love, I believed that there was no other for me and that we would be together forever. During the late summer months, he called me and said that he was moving in with his aunt, which was around the corner from my house. This was great, I thought to myself; I could see him everyday, and I did.

Daily, I spent countless hours with him on the phone. He came over to my house and we watched television together. The kissing and holding of one another became more intense; I allowed him to touch my body, which was a huge deal for me. He was the center of my world and could do nothing wrong. Even if we were in disagreement, he would always side with me and make it right. I knew that he wanted much more than what I was willing to give. I think I watched too much television or listened to too many love songs on how a relationship is supposed to be.

One day, while over at his cousin's house, she and I were talking and she told me the words that any young girl would never want to hear: that he was cheating on me. At that very moment, my heart leaped out of my chest and lay on the floor in plain view. I couldn't move or think; was I embarrassed of what he was doing behind my back? I was stripped of my love at that very moment; the hurt that would transform some years later was commenced. I was scared of the outcome and the thought of being alone again, without someone that I could hear the words I love you from, and the security of being with someone that would never leave me.

I couldn't believe it--the nerve of him cheating on me. Devastated, I confronted him about the situation. He confessed and said that the rumor was true. He said that he was having sex with another girl because I would not have sex with him. He said that he loved me, wanted to be with me, and didn't want to lose me. I could not understand it. I was so torn and hurt over the way that he treated me, after all the things I did for him. I tried to change and save him to make him a better person--and this is what I get for giving and dedicating my time and love to him?

A week had passed and I was in a depression. I didn't know what this feeling was that I had so heavy on my heart. A few days later, he came knocking at my door and said that he loved me, and asked that I take him back. It's easy to say that we would never take a cheater back, but when we have walked in those shoes and we are so emotionally wrapped up in the relationship, our thoughts travel to a different level. After he begged, cried, and said that he would never do it again, I agreed and opened my arms to him, yet again. This time was going to be different. I didn't feel the same way about him. I forced myself to show him attention, but even the simplicity of conversation with him had changed. Although the love was there, it was lacking. Still, I was not sure why I stayed with someone that cheated on me.

The answer seemed quite simple to me. Do we really understand someone if we don't know ourselves, or are these people that we are leaning on replacements for someone else that should have been in our lives?

It's easy for us to develop relationships with people, thinking that they may fill a void and that the companionship is what's missing in our lives, the feeling of loneliness and need for comfort overtakes our path. We think we need someone so badly that we adjust our lives to that feeling. We put our standards on hold and accept what they will give us. Sometimes, we ask for more, just to see what we can get and how long it will last. In the meantime, we have put our standards on hold, and we start to disappear and lose ourselves in someone else.

This transition we will endure only if we allow it to take place. Some of us have already embedded this pattern of self-destruction and don't realize it; general information that is received is often referred to as common sense. Common sense is defined as exhibiting native good judgment. In some cases, we can tend to give the good judgment up because of a person or emotions.

One of the reasons I accepted him back into my life was because I was convinced that I could change him and make him understand that what he did was wrong. So I continued to go though the daily grind; in the back of my mind, I could only think about how he was with that girl. I started to question my belief system and thought that if I had sexual intercourse with him, he would not want anyone else. It seems crazy, but I want you to understand that I linked our lack of sexual activity with our drifting apart. I lost a sense of what the right choice may have been.

Scared Little Black Girl

In time, I realized that I was not happy; because of the trust factor, our relationship became worse and worse. He eventually shut down and stopped expressing his emotions and how he felt about me. I, in turn, made it very difficult to let him forget the mistakes that he made, and would continue to bring it up daily. After about a month, things were not working out anymore, and I had to move on with my life. I decided that he was not worth me having second thoughts about myself. After all, I was a young woman that had her entire life ahead of her.

How Do I Move On?

Before I knew it, it was time to go back to school. My heart was still torn from my dramatic summer, and I did not understand why I was still holding on to the past pain caused by my first love. This year seemed different. I felt that I was growing and understanding who I was becoming. I still knew that I was not ready to have sexual intercourse and stuck to my guns, but it seemed that something was missing in my life. What was I longing for? What was this missing link that was lingering inside of me? Was it the display of affection from my mother and father that I wanted from a relationship with a male? Was it the death of my father, and that there was no other man around to fill his shoes?

Why Did You Leave Me, Daddy?

My father died when I was eight years old, and my mother never remarried until I was almost eighteen. I never got chance to have my first dance with my father or talk to him about a boy. I never got a chance to say goodbye to him and tell him that I loved him face-to-face; I wanted to know him and understand his ideas and thoughts about the way a little girl should be. I received a letter from him before he died. He told me to make sure that I listened to my mother and make sure that my shoes were straight and lined neatly in a row. I tried holding on to all the things that he told me to do. I'm not sure what happened to me that night when my mother received the call from my grandmother that my father had passed away. A piece of me left and I know it, because as I write, I understand my experience: through out life, I looked for the missing piece, that part of me that wondered and wishes and hopes that the man that lay in the coffin on that day was not my father.

I use to daydream and think that it was a mistake they made; they pronounced the wrong man dead. I dreamed that my father, some twenty years later, would appear and say that he was home. That never happened and it never will. The reality of not having answers to many questions left me wondering and analyzing others for their answers, concerns, and thoughts. The pain of losing my father stretched further than I ever imagined, and the magnitude of weight that it would have on me as a young adult moving into womanhood would be greater than I ever imagined.

I can remember the day of the funeral, him lying in the coffin, and my mother falling to her knees, crying and saying, "That's not you, Carmichael." My cousin and aunt grabbed my mother and pulled her away from the coffin. I remember walking up and looking at my father, and touching his ice-cold hands. I looked at the scar that he had on his hand, and said, "Daddy, I love you." I sat back down and looked, as everyone else cried. Not a tear came from my eyes at my father's funeral. I am not sure why I didn't cry. Was I trying to be strong for my mother, or was I a scared little black girl, trying my best to conquer the fear of moving on without my father? Now I question myself and the relationship that I was longing for. Was this the relationship that I had never had with my father? Was I searching for a man that would never leave me, and hurt me the way that my father had hurt me, by dying before I could tell him the things that I needed to say?

I do believe in my heart that most women that don't have a father are searching for love in all the wrong places. The confidence in us is wired differently and it shows. We are a group of women that hold on to dreams of once forgotten love that we missed and wish we had. It can push us in the direction of destruction, if we are not careful. The thing a girl needs from her father is far greater than what anyone can give. The statements, "you look nice today," or "go and take that off; you're not wearing that outfit," are all a part of the molding stage. The voice of a powerful being will cause the little girls to second - guess themselves because of the fear of disappointing their fathers, or make a better choice because it is not the first time they heard a man say that they are beautiful.

By now, school was in session. It was halfway through the year, and in walked a new guy. I thought that he was cute and had potential. That's funny; I don't even know the guy's name, but yet, I already am looking at ways to change him. He played football and was on the wrestling team. He was handsome and strong. After school, during a school activity, he approached me and we started to talk. I discovered that we were both from the same state and had a lot in common. I said to myself: He didn't know about my past relationship. He didn't know that I had my heart broken and crushed by my first love. He didn't know my thought pattern about having sexual intercourse and the type of commitment that I gave my relationships. He didn't know those expectations that I had in mind. I had only talked to him for a couple of days.

A plan is what I called it. This plan will involve all the emotions that I had for my past love, and I will make sure that I release those emotions to him. He will see what kind of person I am. He was completely unaware of the emotional attachment that I exhausted in my previous relationship. I decided to move to this next relationship without giving myself time to heal from the hurt of the summer. Was I truly ready for another relationship? Did I really understand what I wanted from a boyfriend? Did I understand what the word boyfriend really meant?

It is my understanding that we all need someone and we are designed to have a partner at the right time. It is my inclination that we feel the need for the presence of someone to always be around. It gives us cause to jump into relationship after relationship without the necessary time to assess what we are getting out of it. Is there a validation or the appreciation of having a partner that has pledged to you his or her dedication, love, and attention? Do we need to reciprocate what the world taught us and transfer to someone else? Can we take our pain from another situation and unleash it on someone else?

So I met this guy, and he seemed to be the perfect match for me. The same trend happened as it did before: we stayed on the phone talking, going to the movies, going out to eat, and became very close. His mother liked me and my mother adored him; we were great together.

Everyday, I would spend time with him at school and at home. I thought that he was the one for me.

Okay, are you thinking, "did she have sex with this guy?" No, but he introduced me to the sensational feeling of oral sex: oh, what a feeling! He never asked me to perform oral sex on him, and I never did. I can remember the first time he did this to me. I was completely torn for those next few days. After that, did our relationship grow stronger? Or now was it based off of a feeling that we had for one another because of the sensation of touch? We became closer, taking showers together and lying in the bed together naked. He still never pressured me to have sexual intercourse with him. Did he really respect me or did he have a plan?

I was in love again, but it was different this time around. My definition of love was something that two people shared. It was taking long walks, kissing, and holding each other. It was the person buying me gifts and making me feel that I was the center of his world.

But all that love and touching was leading to something that I still was not ready for. I could tell the next school year that the sexual frustration was building up within him. I started to reminisce about my first relationship and what happened when I didn't want to have sexual intercourse. I knew that he was going to do the same thing; after all, isn't that what happens when you don't give a boy what he wants?

Instantly, my emotions came back. It was an immediate reminder of what happened in my first relationship.

Everyday, my heart started to recall the hurt that was hidden and my heart was on the edge of explosion. I began to monitor him at school, analyzing the people that he would talk to. I broke down his body language and time frames. I observed who he was having a conversation with and would make a mental note to confront him later. Our relationship became very intense. I always wanted to be in his presence, because I didn't trust him. For a moment, I thought that I was losing it, thinking that he was doing something behind my back.

It was crazy. I just kept thinking about my first relationship and the impression that I took away from it. I placed the problem in that relationship, using the feeling from the previous as a guide.

I took the feeling I had in one relationship and, instead of letting it go, I bottled all those feelings and buried them. When I looked at my new boyfriend, I saw some of the same qualities and dusted the angry bottle off. Why? I ask myself that same question time and time again. Why would I compare and why would I impose my feelings on someone else that had nothing to do with my past relationship?

In the past, present, and future, we are cowards. We are cowards to those who would hurt us and those that we trust our hearts with. We are cowards to those who know our deepest feelings and become our best friends. Why? In my opinion, our heart and minds have two different agendas, and we are designed to listen to both our hearts and minds.

Scared Little Black Girl

Once we have uncovered the true definition of ourselves, we can determine which to listen to. I chose to listen to my mind at that time; I now know that the tricks of the mind can sometimes be deadly. In my opinion, this is where my emotions stem from. So what is an emotion? This is a feeling that consumes a large part of what we do. This emotion can make us smile, laugh, even venture into another person that we have within us. It is the livelihood of our relationships with people. It helps us to know when and how to react to people, problems, and growing pains. However, a word to the wise: this emotion thesis can also hurt us, rather than help. I believe that as people, we have a certain amount of control. The control we have will play a big part in how we advance in our lives.

When we're in relationships with someone, we will experience the emotions of love and pain. Now each one of us has been though this determining factor and has discovered that at one point or another, each of us will be in love, and at one point or another, each of us will be hurt.

We meet someone and the emotion of love kicks in. We start to think about these people every chance we get. We become lustful and selfish with them, wanting to consume their time and thoughts. We expect them to feel the same way until it doesn't happen the way we anticipated. Then, the pain hits our hearts and those feelings come to life. Now, we realize that these people do not have the same feelings for us and have no interest in meeting us halfway in the relationships. Other feelings surface. The feelings of being imperfect or insecure; questioning ourselves about feelings that we had for this person become present. I think that we are confronted with the pain and love at the same time. We sometimes don't know how to handle the converting of all these emotions.

Yet there is another group that we have not talked about. It is the emotions that are more common in a relationship. They are hate, jealousy, anger, and being selfish. These are the kind of words that are dangerous to us and the people that we're in relationships with. It is my opinion that if we're unable to handle the rejection, the relationship that we thought was love can become pain.

It may sound like I was some type of stalker with this guy, but I had an excuse, I told myself. After all, he touched me like no other, and kissed me like none else had. I allowed him to caress my body. It was his touch that I became accustomed to. And because of this, I felt I had the right to have control over him, myself, and how we should feel about each other. Time passed us by, and the pattern of spending time together every weekend, whether watching a movie or just sitting in the house, became a part of my routine.

Two years passed in the relationship and still, no sexual intercourse with each other took place. The pressure was on. The relationship was sinking because I was not interested in putting out. We started to have problems. He didn't want to spend time with me anymore. He said that I was not willing to commit to having sex with him. The arguments came more and more frequently; we grew apart. There was nothing that I could do about it. We still spent some time together, but it wasn't the same. The connection we had was fading fast, but despite what he was saying, I still wanted him in my life.

Our arguments became altercations. We would physically fight and he would restrain me. Finally, I was getting his attention. My words and body was not enough anymore, so I created situations and he had no choice but to give me the attention that I desired. The negative attention got the best of us. We were tired of the arguments and hanging up on each other, but we stayed in the relationship, unhappy.

Yeah, you guessed it: he was cheating. I don't know if I can really say cheating and be completely truthful. I can't seem to understand how you can cheat on someone and not be fully committed. We say that we should only be with one person, but if we're in a relationship and our partner is not making us happy, does it give us the right to go behind their backs and sleep with someone else? Is this a lack of respect for the trust that we have given that person?

Part of me says I can't blame him, but I did. He was the villain in this film, and I was the flawless queen, never doing anything to deserve this. I was just the perfect angel. I was seventeen now, and I had had two bad relationships that both ended with the same results. Hurt and devastated, I tried my best to make sure that it would never happen to me again. I didn't know what was wrong. Did I see something in my immaturity that was making my relationships unsuccessful? Was I trying something that I was not ready for and could not accept the reality of it?

I had an issue, at this point, with trust. I found myself questioning family, friends, and any male that I would come in contact with. Once I had been damaged, it was hard to undo. I had bad memories that would not go away. They stuck with me; I carried them from relationship to relationship.

Now What?

Depending on the type of relationship that we experience, it's not uncommon for us to go into a trance, a state of altered consciousness; a hypnosis can affect us and make us become distant from ourselves and others. This will cause us to go into isolation. This isolation phase is a continuous effort to exclude ourselves from our problems and others that encourage us to move in a different direction.

Do we hold ourselves back from progressing and detaching ourselves from emotions of hurt and pain? Do we give ourselves enough time before we move on, and begin to release the pain to join in new relationships?

I'm not able to answer that question for someone else. People have suggested it can take about a year to get over someone that we have been with, either good or bad. This is the opinion-based information of one saying that a healing process can vary in each individual relationship and person. If we don't give ourselves time to get ready to present ourselves to another relationship, we'll find ourselves not understanding how to handle a new one.

In fact, because of your mental state, it is more likely that the person you have decided to be involved with becomes the person that you fall in love with before it's even true. The attachment to the other person has not healed, so you cling to the new person as if they were the old. More than likely, this new person will have traits that your old mate had. However, there may be some improvements.

For example, your old mate may have had a drinking problem and gone out all the time. This was a big issue in your last relationship. In fact, it was one of the main reasons why you broke up. In your mind, you make some exception, saying, "I will accept that he goes out, but I won't accept the drinking." Your new mate does go out sometimes, but doesn't like to drink a lot. In your mind, you have made some big improvements, but it's only by a small measure that the change in characteristic is different. This will end with the same results.

My thought is that you revert back to your comfort zone, which is a place that is familiar to you. This comfort zone guarantees that you will stay safe, which is somewhat the same as putting your guard up. We all have experienced this in our lives. It is how we cope with the things that don't go right, but return to a similar situation because we know the end results.

Have you ever experienced this issue? How did you handle it? Were you able to move from one relationship to another without bringing the other emotional attachments? Or was it difficult for you to accept someone else without connecting them to the other person? Think about the word compare; what does it mean to you? The definition is to be similar or a complete match.

We all do it, nick for knack; we compare apples to apples, to see what the end result will be. So we take a little bit of our old person and intertwine them with the new. Even though the old is no longer there, we self-consciously think they are. The outcome is a made-up person that we think is the perfect match for us, and will not hurt us this time around.

It's almost like we're playing a game with ourselves to see who will become the winner. So now hurt, love, and pain become weapons of revenge and destruction without us understanding or identifying them as that. Instead, we ignore painful behavior and block the right way of doing things, which turn into a first-degree felony of shame. The only people we're incarcerating are ourselves and our trains of thought.

I guess we have to step back, and ask ourselves when we are aware of this behavior pattern created. The answer you only know. Over my lifetime, I have experienced that even though I know that there is an issue, and other people bring it to my attention, the only person that can change the direction of my life is me. Once we have realized there's a problem, we try to change for the better and try not revert back to the worst.

For me, by now, I was done with relationships. I started to hang around people who were not faithful and was just looking to hang out and have fun. After all, I was in high school and had been involved in serious relationships for the first three years. It was time to have fun and enjoy the other things that high school had to offer. Still priding myself on being a virgin, I used it as a tool to get what I wanted from males.

I played a hell of a game with them, so I thought. It was one of a kind. Have you ever met someone that you really wanted to be with and would do anything to be around or with that person? Have you ever met someone you wanted to hold, touch, and just have a simple conversation with? I knew that one thing that men wanted was an untouched woman. They wanted to say that I was the first one. They wanted to have bragging rights to get the "draws," and as they used to say, "pop the cherry." It was more important and it meant ownership over that person for life. To be able to have an untouched person and turn them into something different meant empowerment and rules were put in place.

So trying my best, I became a guy in a sense. I started to think with my mind and not my emotions; I became that paper bag that would conform to all purposes and not be torn. I mastered the game of being "a player." This player sense was ridiculous, but it made the days go by and was fun for me. Without committing to any relationship, I established communication with one guy after another, dating, talking on the phone, kissing, and even sometimes making emotional outpours that were not true. I even sometimes made myself cry, just to see how they would react to certain situations. It was amazing to see how people reacted to emotions; some cared and others just pushed back, not knowing what to do.

This was an adventure for me. I could not believe that all of these guys were interested, and that all of them wanted a piece of me. I knew that if they got a piece, all the hard work they dedicated would end. Some would stick around for a while; the others felt they worked for it and walked away with the reward. It was almost like vultures flying over me and waiting for the right time.

I knew what the game plan was. I knew that they were lining up at the door, and as soon as the opportunity presented itself, they were going to swoop down and go for the kill. I was smarter than that and my indication was that life itself had more to offer than just a whole lot of boys wanting to get me in the bed.

Now I know what you're thinking–"yeah, right, you had to have sex with some of them." Yes, you're right; I did. Because of what my last boyfriend introduced me to, most of the guys that I was in contact with preformed oral sex on me. I never returned the favor; let me make sure I put that out there. I found out that if you play the cards right, a guy will do just about anything when he is working on meeting a goal.

I always respected myself, not letting them feel all over me, and was under the impression that I was not abusing my body. I assumed, because I was not having actual sexual intercourse, that I was a virgin. I was a virgin in my mind, but I wasn't a virgin, someone that is in a pure and natural state. Therefore, although a virgin from a copulating standpoint, I was not completely untouched.

So I deemed myself as one, but the emotional got-to-have-it feeling was there. I had to have that connection with a male caressing my one body part in that way. Why? Because I had been introduced to it, it became a pattern that never ended. It became a lifestyle that was a continuous requirement that any male that I connected with had to be able to meet the requirements of my sexual preference. There were some guys that rejected, and decided to move on. Other guys were okay with the idea, again, thinking that it would pay off.

Oh, it was a feeling that I can't describe to know that every guy wanted me in that way. It was a feeling that made me understand what men were about, and what they desired from women. But was it the right desire? Was this an entrapment of something that could potentially become harmful? Was this a practice that would lead into infatuation and patterns of unforgivable love? Was this feeling from some type of void in my life that I was unaware of?

So, at this point in my life, I was creating a pattern of seduction and mental abuse, and I thought that it was fun. What could I do next? The player thing started to get old and the guys started to get attached. They wanted to be around me more and more; I was losing control of them. They were attacking from all angles different agendas.

I think that when you start to twist em confuse people, the mind game is really wit start to underestimate the power of mental control and the emotional responsibility that we have. We become confused ourselves, along with confusing others. When do we begin to take the responsibility for hurting people and help to repair their hearts? When do we take ownership of our actions, and apologize for the things that we knowingly have done to hurt, because we thought that it was cute, funny, or would prove a point? When do we come to our heads and understand that people hurt and feel like we do, every day and night? It's those times we are responsible for creating a bad memory that may stick with people for a lifetime, and alter some of their life choices.

I think that when we're hurting, we often want others to be able to feel that same pain, and because we can not physically give our pain that we are feeling to people, we transfer it by placing them in the same situation that we were in and hurting them the way that love hurt us.

We all want to strive to be the best that we can be, whether it is in our friendships, relationships, jobs, or sports. We always want to come out the winner and be number one. We need to be that person that is looked at as a winner. This is the same person who sets an example for his family or roommates--the perfect person.

So, I ask you, "Are you that person who does everything right? Have you hurt anyone and felt a sense of achievement at another person's expense? Have you transferred your feeling of insecurity, self-pity, and infatuation onto another person? Have you not passed judgment on someone, making them to be something more or less than what they are? Do you know in your heart, at one point in your life, whether it was as a child, sister, bother, mother, father, aunt, uncle, grandmother, or grandfather, what opinion you have given to someone?

Now, are you sorry in any way? Are you remorseful? Do you care about how you affected someone else, or is it just one of those things? Ask yourself those questions and answer with honesty and integrity. This question to be answered cannot come from anyone else; it must and has to come from ourselves. Can and when will we hold ourselves accountable and be honest with ourselves, grow and trust to respect the souls, minds, and hearts that we come in contact with daily? We are impacting without even giving thought of what the outcome will be. What may be worse is that we will wonder to ourselves if we should even care.

Honest stands for truthful, trustworthy, judging by a fair means. Can you determine in your past how and what define your reputation?

But the questions still remains: are you a person that has committed a homicide, the killing of a person by another? We are going to use this as the killing of someone's spirit, drive, and determination to become what they should be in life. You can commit homicide without doing bodily harm. How? By the words that come out

Scared Little Black Girl

of your month, body language, facial expressions, and attitude, and by misrepresenting to someone his self worth, when he doesn't know it, but you do. You see, people can see things in other people that we sometimes can't see in ourselves. When you have a person that understands the potential in you, and they don't understand the potential in themselves, they seek to destroy all that they come in contact with, tearing them down brick by brick and consuming our minds to get us on the level of disbelief.

Is it humanly possible? Pay attention to the signs of these people watching you, almost as if they are crawling around you like a bug that you can't see. You almost are being micromanaged by this person, a mischievous decision that you are not conscious of. This is you killing the person not by a physical death, but an emotional one. Mentally, this damage can be more fatal than a physical attack with a gun.

Or, are you one of the rare individuals that is of honor, high regards, respect, and a high reputation? Are you a person who uplifts individuals? Do you reverse your roles, and are you able to give them knowledge and enable them to go to new horizons? Are you encouraging them to believe that they are worthy and have a higher power within themselves that they have not yet uncovered? Do you have a special understanding of some of the tactics of the world, people who they will encounter and who will uplift them in a positive light, by giving the encouraging words that are in your mind, body, and spirit? Can you be that person they come and cry to, and understand their immediate needs? Are you that person who places his own selfish ways to the back burner? Are you a person that puts his own thoughts aside, and consume the information being presented to him?

Who Are You?

Well, tell the truth! We all wish that we could be this honest person. The truth of the matter is that there is a mixing in the bowl. It is a mixing of homicide and honesty. A mixing means being composed of different parts, classes, races, and confusion. It is not uncommon; in fact, there are people by the masses who have this issue. The word mass is the quantity of matter or the size. People just don't understand the destruction we have caused to ourselves and other people that surround us everyday.

So, I caution and advise; the next time you talk to someone, we should determine if it is a homicide or a honest statement that you are making.

I know for myself that I was all mixed up with the different issues. I would love to love, and then start to hate people because they did not conform to my rules. If men didn't want to perform that sexual favor or give me what I wanted, I deemed them deserving to be hurt. If they were on the list, I said, let the games begin.

I would say sweet words to them and caress their minds, which would give an indication that I was head-over-heels for them. Sometimes, I would even buy them something and make them feel like they were a special person in my life. I would do things, and call often, even when I didn't want to talk. I would give them the sense that I was really interested, and seem as if I was falling in love. Whispering sweet things over the phone and telling them to be my first was a common activity. Lifting them with words of encouragement and honor, as if they were the man of my dreams, was a tactic.

I was very careful to make sure that none of the tricks that I was playing flipped on me. Many of us have pretended before. I'm not the only person who has played this song and dance game. In fact, my guess is that others are even better than I am. I felt so confident in the ability to deceive that it became the way of living, pleasing and having fun. A back-stabbing is what I called it. The games eventually became a part of me, and I didn't know how to break it. Even when I would meet someone that seemed to be right, I reverted back to what I was used to doing. I closed my heart to affection and reacted with the impulses of the thrill, of not being the one hurt.

I was tired of playing the game, and wanted to have a relationship with someone that cared. At eighteen, we think of opportunities available in the world. We seek out and we are blind to the facts. Perhaps we don't know what to look for. Now, I am aware of the opportunities and choices that we have to make. These activities can be negative or positive, depending on what we choose.

Unfortunately, most of the decisions that we make when we're young are wrong, but seem right. I believe that if we don't ever make wrong choices, we'll never understand what is right. We have to bump our heads and learn, or we will have a hard time leading ourselves and anyone else on the right track. I'm not saying that if we make right choices we're wrong, or that we'll never be leaders. I'm saying that a great percentage of us may go in the wrong direction, because we don't pull from the source that has been provided for us since before we were born.

I had a conversation with a person once that told me someone's eyes can tell you a story. I challenge most of my friends to do this every so often. I give you the same challenge, of being observant and taking in your surroundings. Go into a store and take a look around. We see plenty of people: women, children, husbands, and wives. Notice a few couples that are in the store. Some seem to be very happy. Now focus a little more.

Based on some of my own personal observations, I'm asking you to take a look at the children in most situations. They seem to be cared for, clean and healthy, happy, not sad, and in most cases, cheerful and playful. Take a look at the husband; he may not take the best care of his body; however, he seems to be clean-cut and well put together. When you look into his eyes, you may not see the stress and worry that is weighing on the family. Now take a look at the woman; this woman is holding it all together, not just for herself, but for the children, the husband, and a number of other people who are not in your immediate sight. As you get closer, you can almost feel her from across the room, longing for the sensitive attention that is necessary to keep her going day to day. Now take an even closer look; what do you see? If you look into her eyes, you can see the fears, loneliness, worry, unhappiness, distrust, anger, attitude, self-control, ambition, and courage. Depending on your internal sense, what can be obvious to you may not be apparent to another. Don't prejudge people because they look a certain way; but the reality of a feeling or a dismissed emotion coming from a woman, man, or child is something that I tend to be dawn to.

The description of the woman tells me that she is not giving herself enough fuel to satisfy everyone throughout the day, including herself. It goes unnoticed for weeks, months, and unfortunately, years, until she is unable to take it anymore. This example is just not with this woman; the example is in you. The husband and even the children can carry this same burden.

Ask yourself what people see when they look at you from across the room.

Do they see a broken down person?
Do they see a person who has confidence?
Do they see a potential leader?
Do they see a failure?
Do they see an example?
Do they see your past?

Scared Little Black Girl

Do they see your future?
Do they see your stress?
Do they see your frustration?
Do they see your joy?
Do they see your anger?
Do they see your disappointments?
Do they see your journey?
Or,
Can they see your goodness?
Can they see your heart?
Can they see your attitude?
Can they see you for who you are?

Do you care? Should we care about how someone else views us, or how someone else is affected by us? Do we think about how someone else can relate to us, or about how we can affect someone else? Do we impact things that they do around us, and not only affect what they do around us, but affect what they will do around another person as a result of being around us? It's almost like a chain reaction that affects one thing after another.

Most of what we do in life is because we see someone else doing it. Something may spark our attention and other activities, views, and events may not. When we look at something that we like, our minds start to fantasize about how we would look doing that or how that would look on us. At times, we can even imagine what we would do, if we were there, and how great we would be at it. Without realizing it, this person that we were observing has had an influence on us. This person has set an example, even if we have not made it our goal to do what they are dong. They have made an impression on us; whether we set it as a goal immediately, or it lays a deferred dream.

After focusing on what other people are doing, do you stop to think that someone is also focused on you? Do people look at our lifestyles and try to mimic them? Are they thinking that it's okay to be a participant in the activities that we are engaged in? I've asked myself the same questions time and time again.

I mentioned that I was trying to be a player. This was not something that I intended to do. It was established years and years ago, and each generation defines it differently. This concept of being a player was a replicated action that I received from someone else. I watched and learned as many of us do. I was taking lesson from the sideline without the notebook in hand, walking alongside, listening to the way they would talk, dress, and laugh. I observed the environment which they allowed themselves to be surrounded by, their acts, and the company they kept. It was almost like someone had taken all the information they had and placed it within my body. It takes a lot of work to imitate someone. This means that every move and conversation has now become a routine to you as well.

The truth about the matter is that all of us have done this at some point in our lives. It is called being influenced by our peers. It is wanting to try something new that we have never done before, wanting to understand the excitement that others have experienced and felt, wanting to see if we can accomplish the same goals that they did, and making this a system of competition. It could be wanting an understanding of the feeling of joy from accomplishing what someone else had done, or maybe it was just wanting to have bragging rights that we're better than someone else.

For me, it was the bragging rights, and the fact that I could say, "I did that before and was good at it." I was good at making someone believe the unbelievable, making them experience something that was not true. I made them think they were the keys to my dreams and that losing them would be devastating for me.

I came to realize after a while that I was not only tricking them, but had begun to trick myself as well. Many times when we're lying, we have to start to believe what we're saying or we'll get lost in our lies. We're making up our own stories, but we don't know the endings to the stories. Once we have started to believe in the things that we are saying to someone else, they become dangerous. Our feelings and focus to make that person believe everything we say gets lost, and we trick ourselves in the end. Ultimately, we come to a place where we become unhappy, because we have created this world of emotions that are based on lies. We cannot control these lies any longer, and they become who we are and what other people know us to be.

What I found out is that once we're in it, the mistakes and life lessons begin to happen. We find that our mates are not compatible, and it starts to become a reality that we are not happy. Our lies start to repeat, except now, our feelings are involved and we can't decipher what is true.

My experience turned out to be painful, unwanted, and revealing of who I was at that time in my life. I knew that all I had to do was to deceive people into believing that they were something that they were not. So, I did.

After high school, a turn happened in my life. All of a sudden, my fun and games ended with a quick announcement from my mother. After being single for over fifteen years, my mother announced that she was married. There was no warning; no one knew that she was in love, and because of that, things changed. I found myself on the day of my graduation moving my mother's things into a new house with her husband, and I was not invited. I remember it like it was yesterday; my mother took me shopping for my graduation outfit. I picked out this beige dress with flower-like beige shoes. I went home to pull up to the U-Haul truck, which I helped pack, and slipped on my graduation clothes and walked across the stage.

Lost and at a dismay, I had to make rash decisions that would lead to a lifetime of pain and lessons that I knew I was not ready to encounter. The fun and games were over, and now it was time for me to grow up, face responsibility, and take care of myself, and that's exactly what I did.

The day of graduation—alone, unhappy, and a scared little black girl—I agreed with a friend who was going through the same situation as me that we would work and make the best of a bad situation by moving from home to home and trying to make the best choices. Although I didn't have a place to call home, that didn't stop me from trying my best to survive.

I met a guy, and although I didn't like him, my mind told me to go ahead. What I mean by that is that my mind allowed me to focus on what was in it for me. This guy was not flashy, and didn't have the best clothes or car, but somehow, I knew I could depend on him. We went out a few times, talked, kissed, and that was about it. He always seemed to care, and so, I decided that I would act like I cared, too. After moving from place to place, finally having nowhere to stay, I came to him with tears in my eyes one day. My mother had her new husband and did not have the time or energy to handle the emotional drama of a teenager. I asked my sister if I could stay with her and she agreed, only to have her husband reject the idea. I was alone; I had nowhere to go. I thought to myself, what am I going to do now? As a last resort, I went to my cousin's house; my cousin lived nearby, and she agreed to let me stay with them for a while.

Unfortunately, at that time in my life, I was not open to anyone advising me on anything. I lived in the house with them. My twelve-year-old cousin thought that she was "big stuff." While watching television late one night, my cousin turned the channel, which made me upset. I got up and pushed her through the closet, making a large hole in my aunt's apartment. Around 2:00 a.m., my aunt said that I had to go. I packed the small things I had in my bag and called him on the phone. Within the hour, he came and picked me up. I was not sure what I was going to do, because I had no place to go. He told me that I should not worry, and that he would ask his mother if I could stay with his family.

Devastated, I went with him, approaching his mother's house. I could not focus on anything, and would have peed in my pants if I had been startled. We exited the car and walked into this house. The house was an old home with an odd, yet homey smell. His mother and stepfather were asleep. He told me to have a seat in the living room. I sat and very quietly thought to myself that I would get myself out of this situation. He went and woke up his mother, and she came into the living room. I looked at her and recognized that she had been where I was about to go. She asked me my name, and I told her. I complimented her on her house a few times, very nervously. She asked me questions about my family. I explained to her that my mother, sister, and aunt didn't want me to live with them, and that I had been living door-to-door for quite some time. I told her that I really liked her son, and that I would only stay for a while.

Oh, dear mother agreed that I could stay for a while, and that's what I intended to do. I had a short-term plan that would allow me to save money and go to school. I still had my acceptance letters to a few colleges, and was short five hundred dollars of going to Central State University. Kindness of a gentle hand became an obligation of deceit. By now, all my belonging were gathered from all of my

Scared Little Black Girl

homes, and I moved in with him. As the nights became darker and darker, my fear of something happening that I was not ready for grew closer and closer. On a warm summer night, I could hear the crickets as we walked into the house. We went to the second floor, in the attic of the house, and although I had been here many times before, this summer night marked a new experience. He held my hand and guided me up the dark steps, and I followed up him until we reached the door of the room. As he opened the door, I heard a loud crack, as if it had not been open for years. It was an unfamiliar place to me; at that time, I felt displaced and concerned about what would happen next. It was cold and seemed to have an old-smelling odor. On the floor was a pallet of some covers, and little else but some clothes and shoes. He sat down beside me and we started to talk. We talked about what I was going to do with my life. I recited sweet dreams of mine to go to college and become a lawyer, and that I was just around five hundreds dollars short of having the admissions to a major college. I expressed to him that I was trying to make something of myself.

I often wonder, if the light had been on, would he have seen the fear in my eyes, or would he have even cared? As I sat, he walked around the room, talking and staring at me. I continued talking to him, wishing that I could leave and never come back, but I knew in my mind that he was after more than just a conversation. He stood in front of me and then sat beside me. I saw something in him at that very moment, that feeling of making someone become afraid and intimidating them to do what you want them to do. In the blink of an eye, his conversation turned the other way, and he began to touch me and say things to me that I could not bear to hear, words of lust and desire to do things to my body that I was not ready for. Frightened, my hands began to shake and sweat dripped from my forehead. My body became numb as he started to touch my hair, and his breath of beer and cigarettes infested my skin. The thought of him kissing me with his lips made my stomach turn, and I felt as if I was losing my breath and wanted to turn and run, but my legs could not move. He moved closer to me, and I felt his hands go up my shirt; he whispered in my ear, "Are you ready?" I replied yes, and he laid me down. At that very moment, I left my body and looked at me with discuss and embarrassment. I hated my mom at that very second. How could she do this to me? How could she release me to the world without preparing me for the horrible thing that was going to happen to me? This man took my body and did what he wanted, as I laid limp, and the tears flowed down my eyes. I felt as if someone had splashed hot water on my face from the heat and redness that I'm sure was on my face. His touch was like a snake, slithering on my skin, leaving the slime on my body. As he climbed on top of me, I was being raped. I didn't enjoy his touch, and the combination of alcohol and smoke made me sick. He asked if I was ready. I nodded my head, and said yes. Yes, to what he wanted to do, so that I would have a place to stay. Yes, to having a hot meal and a place to lay my head; yes, to making sure that I did not have to go door-to-door anymore. I said yes to not having to find someone that would take me in. Yes, to a sense of peace, and hoped I made the best decision for me. He climbed off me, and I turned my body around and felt as if I wanted to kill myself and make it all go away. I realized that everything I believed in went out the door, and I just became another girl that did an injustice to her body and spirit. As he gathered his clothing, he got up and walked to the other side of the room and began to smoke a cigarette, as if he had won some great war and that this was the prize, my worth, breaking me in, teaching me a lesson, showing me that he knew how to have sex and that I was some great thing that proved himself. He was sitting with a smirk on his face, making sure that I noticed, and throwing the emotions in my face.

How could this be? I've been saving myself all this time for someone special, and was this him? I asked myself, over and over again, wondering what I would do now. Now that I was not a virgin, and someone had my touch, emotional, and mental state altered, what was I going to do? The next day, I awoke in a daze. Denial is what I determined it to be. I couldn't believe that it came down to this. Was this even worth it?

I turned and looked at him, knowing that I didn't love him or care about him. He didn't love me, either. The reward that he received from me was far greater than he would ever imagine. So, I sat and sat and made myself believe that he was in love with me and that I loved him, too. In my mind, I formed a perception of him being someone that he was not, and that he was unaware of all the things he was capable of. I desired to know that we were going to be together, forever, because I had had sex with him. After all, he did tell me he loved me and took me in when no one else would.

When I looked at him, I noticed that he was at peace with the choice he made to lead me up the stairs that night and lay me on the floor. I knew that he was at peace with himself, asking his mother if I could move in, and knowing that he would be the first man in my life to take my sexuality to another level. I knew that he was at peace with taking that precious part of me and turning it into something that he wanted it to be, to say that he was the first person, to say that he was the one to make me into a so-called woman. He was able to say that he won the prize, and that's exactly what he did. He told everyone that he had sex with me and that he was the first one. People that I never would have talked to knew that I was no longer a virgin. He spread the news as if it was an epidemic; sharing about me and how he had me.

I was ashamed and embarrassed to show my face. I was an advocate for not having premarital sex. This is one of the things that I lived for. I knew that I would have to be brave and live up to what I had done, not only for myself, but for the people who were looking at me and forming an opinion of me. I took some time to myself to reflect on the situation that occurred. I was alone with the thoughts of what happened that night. I didn't find it as special as I thought that it would be. I had never felt a hand, touch, or kiss like that. Instead, I felt dirty and tricked into a situation that was unreal and a world I was not ready to discover. Thinking of what happened that night, I remembered his touch, which felt like he had a glove on, with a rough feeling to my flesh: indescribable cold, unwanted and self-sacrificed touch of deceitfulness, and frustration of his past, present, and future. I wanted to forget and make it all go away. I wished that I could go back to sleep and make it all disappear, but I knew that was not going to happen. I felt regret in my heart; my mind told me that I did the right thing, but my heart told me different.

It never dawned on me to try to understand what this person was like when he was angry, or when he was happy or all the other habits that followed. I was so worried about how this could benefit me that I never calculated the equation of how this would hurt me.

Living with someone on a day-to-day basis is something different from being boyfriend and girlfriend that live with their parents. It becomes like a simulated marriage. This so-called marriage consists of a few given factors. It involves giving yourself 100 percent of the time to that person. I'm not only referring to sexual intercourse. I'm talking about excluding yourself to make someone else happy and content with you and your surroundings. You don't just give yourself to them, but to their family and friends. Everyone gets a piece of you. It seems funny and unbelievable, but to those people that are living with a man or woman: you can relate. For those of you that don't understand, let me break it down.

So you meet this guy, and because he loves you, you love him. He and you decide to try each other out. You move in together to get a sample of how life would be with one another. This sample consists of a few different elements:

1. Family: the family puts you though this test to see if you are the right person for their son or daughter. During a family event, different people approach you to feel you out. The mother may ask you to cut the turkey; brothers and sisters may ask you to run them to the store. What are they looking for? Well, they want to see if you are a good match for the family. They want to know if you're smart or have the will power to say no. They want to know if you have selfish ways and if you would be able to help the family out in the event that the family runs into a situation. Do they really want to know if you care about their daughter or son? In most cases, yes, but they also want to know what's in it for them.

2. Friends: your friends will do the same thing as your family, but this time, it is a little different; sure, they are happy you found someone; sure, they want you to have a great life and marry the person of your dreams; but what are their motives? When they meet you, they want to observe you and find out if you know anyone they know, just so they can find out a little more information to report back to their friends,

Scared Little Black Girl

about what they have heard about you. You have to understand that the friends' perception of you can be of great worth, depending on the type of relationship that they have with their friends. If you are now a part of their friends' lives, you can almost become a threat to them. So now you are in a battle for attention--the attention that was once directed to them and now is being directed to you.

Now you have a clear understanding that you are not in a relationship with just this woman/man; you are in a relationship with the entire surrounding of their lifestyles. Many of us go into relationships because we think it's fun, or we just didn't make the right choices and are not brave enough to back away. Now that the family and friends have decided to accept or reject you, you're still stuck in this sample live-in situation.

This live-in marriage, so-called relationship, can become very difficult. You have to be a certain kind of person to be able to deal with someone that is not your husband, but you deal with him or her as if they are. This is deep to me, because you almost can program yourself to become this person that you should not be.

In my case, there were many duties that I performed. I worked, cleaned, cooked, paid the bills, and had to please him all at the same time, trying to find out who I was, while completing my daily assigned tasks. I didn't love him when we moved in together, so it became somewhat of a chore to do on a day-to-day basis, including having sexual intercourse. I had no feeling, and at times, would lay there and wish that I was somewhere else--on a beach, or in a class, learning. It never was great for me, because I never knew that love was meant to be something different. So daily I said yes to him, yes to him climbing on top of me, yes to him mistreating me, yes to him not coming home at night, and yes to him not making me happy. I know what you're thinking: why would you stay with someone you didn't love? Why not move out after you got a job and get your own place? It sounds so simple, doesn't it, but the realty is that when you are eighteen and alone, with little or no understanding of who you are, you don't know what to do. You can't handle every situation that comes your way, so you cope with it the best way you know how, until you figure it out. You let someone become an influence over your life and over your decisions. Some of their choices become yours, and their habits take precedent over yours. In most cases, you start to mimic what they do, say, and feel, cooking and cleaning and trying to make the best out of a bad situation.

After all, I thought to myself that he was the only one who cared about me enough to give me a place to live, and the only one that was giving me the support to keep me going at this time in my life.

Then the unthinkable happened—yes, I was pregnant. Imagine that: just thinking that this live-in thing was hard enough--now what was I going to do? I could barely take care of myself, and I didn't want to be with him at least for much longer. Now this put a hold on my plans. I thought that I would seek the advice of others to help me though this problem. I instantly went to talk to my sister, who had been in a bad marriage and had a son already, which she had been taking care of all by herself. My sister called my mother, and they both had their input. While I was waiting over at my sister's house to talk to both my mom and sister, he showed up at the door. My gosh, I thought to myself, everyone in here knows that I've had sex.

Instantly, my sister said that he would not be there for me. He would leave and I'd be left raising the baby alone. My mom said that I was too young to have a child, and I needed to think about my options. My mom said that if I kept the baby, he and I should get married, because it was the right thing to do. I told my mother no, I would not get married to someone just because I was pregnant. I looked at him and he defended his point and position. He said the words that any scared and alone child would want to hear. He told my mom and sister that he loved me, and that he wanted to be with me; he said that no matter what, he would be with me and take care of this child and me. Needless to say, I took his word for it. The confusion started in my sister's house. My sister pleaded with me to get an abortion, and said that she would pay for the procedure. She said that I had a bright future and I shouldn't let some guy ruin it before I even had a chance to live. She said that he would say those things to me because he wanted me to have a child, and that he would not be there. He argued back at her, and said that she was judging him to be wrong, and that again, he cared for me, and he had proved it already, by taking care of me and making sure that I had a place to live and food to eat. The angry cloud was in that room that night, but I went into a daze and had to think about what to do. It was evident that the decision that was to be made could only be made by me.

My mind was made up. I was going to keep my child and do the best that I could to support him or her. After all, my sister was doing it by herself, and she seemed to have it under control. My mother did it by herself and took in two additional kids, and did it on her own after my father passed away. It didn't seem that hard to take care of another person. I thought to myself that I had been watching my nephew for some time and didn't have a hard time doing that. After all, I was not going to have to do it by myself; he said that he would always be there for me. I had no reason to doubt him, because he had taken care of me up until this point.

That night, after we left my sister's house, we went home. I was still stressed from the fact that I would be having a baby soon. I didn't understand the amount of responsibility and the pain that I was going to encounter. The next few weeks passed, and I became very ill. I called one of my friends, and she said that I should go see the doctor, so that I could get pregnancy treatments. I agreed, and she picked me up and took me to the doctor. While waiting for my appointment, I talked to my friend, who was pregnant also, and she said that she was aborting her baby, and said that I should do the same. She told me that she was not ready to have a baby, because she didn't have all the things she needed in order to take care of it. I told her that I was trying to make the best choice for me and my unborn child, and I thought that I could handle it.

Finally, the doctor called me back and took me to the examination room. Because I had never had sex with anyone, I'd never had a pap smear. This meant the doctor had to conduct a vaginal exam. So the doctor prepared to do this, and could not proceed with the process. He stood up, looked at me, and said, "I don't know how you got pregnant; you were not penetrated." The doctor then said that he was going to have to insert a small cut in order for him to proceed on to the next procedure. I looked at my friend and said that I was scared, and she looked at me and said that she was scared, too. We were two young girls that didn't have a clue what sex meant and all the things that it brought. The doctor came back into the room with the nurse and a small knife, and asked me to lie down on the table. My friend grabbed my hand and told me that it would be okay. I looked at her and held on to her as if this was the last time I would see her.

As the doctor approached the table, my legs begin to tremble, and I felt nerves twitch in my stomach. The suspense of the pain that was coming was too intense to handle. At that moment, I wanted my mother to hold my hand like she used to when I fell down and scraped my knee. I knew that she was not going to walk in the door, but wished that she would have. The nurse with deep brown eyes looked into my eyes and said that it was going to be okay. The doctor proceeded to approach the table, telling me to relax. I knew the pain was coming, and I started to tense up. The very thought of someone cutting me in a place where I'd never been touched made me want to grab my belongings and leave at that very moment. The doctor cut and the pain was intense; I cried and screamed, and the nurse rubbed me and assured me that it was alright. I never felt pain like that before, and knew that I never wanted to feel pain like that again. The doctor put some bandages on me, then stated that I should not have sex for a while, and started me on the pills to have a healthy baby. I left the doctor's office with second thoughts. I didn't know if I was making the right or wrong choice. I knew that I could not take the pain, and needless to say, he was not at the doctor appointment with me. I felt it was no big deal for him not to go to the hospital with me, but I didn't realize how much that should have meant. The doctor told me that I could not do much and that I needed to rest for most of the pregnancy.

Still not completely convinced that I was making the best decision, that night, I flipped though the yellow pages, searching for clinics to have an abortion, and called my sister again. My sister said that she would take me, and that I had a choice. I had a choice to go to college and become someone; I had a choice to be able to be in love at the right time with the right person; I had a choice to take another road in life and not the same path that she had taken, and that she wanted something better for me. I explained that I didn't want to make anyone unhappy, and that I wanted to make the best decision. I didn't know what to do. I had no job and no form of transportation. My sister said that I needed to think about the choices that I was making, and to make sure that it was what I wanted to do and, not what anyone else wanted.

The following day, I marked some of the places that I wanted to call. They said that the cost would be around three hundred dollars, and that I would have to have all the money up front. They said that the procedure would kill the baby, and they would give me a method of birth control to prevent me from getting pregnant again. I still didn't know what to do. I wanted to go to school and wanted to make something of myself. I was living with his mother and step-father, so during this time, I had a conversation with his mother. His mother sat me down and said that she had been in my situation before, and that she understood that I wanted to do things in life. His mother said that she and the family would help me with the baby, and that I could stay with them as long as I needed to, until I was on my feet. She said that I could go to school and that she and the family would be there to help support the baby. I listened to her, and took the information that she gave and tried to make the right choice.

I sat and sat and sat, and reflected on the conversations that I'd had with my mother, sister, friends, and his mother, and made up my mind that I would move on and have the baby.

Two months into the pregnancy, I couldn't eat, sleep, or even get out of bed. I was throwing up day and night, and hadn't imagined this type of pain. I never had been this sick, even when I'd had the flu as a little girl. Meanwhile, while I was sick, this so-called boyfriend was out in the streets. He said that he was making money; he said that he was over his friend's house; he said that he wanted to hang out at the clubs; he said that he could do what he wanted to do, and he could, but I couldn't. I couldn't hang out at the club and do as I pleased; my friends had moved on and gone to school, and in the meantime, here I was, stuck with a baby in my stomach and the drama of this so-called man that was really a boy. I couldn't come home in the middle of the night, go back out, and stay out all night. I couldn't have it my way, and also be pregnant and sick at the same time.

Disgusted, in a rage, he said that he wanted me to have the baby, but was never home to comfort me and help me though the situation. I was alone and afraid of the decision that I had made. Now, just around four months into the pregnancy, the sickness was still bad and his attitude was worse. He took on this personality that he was who he was and that no one was going to change him. I couldn't believe it! What a mess I'd gotten myself into, and now I didn't know how to get out of it. I cried day and night, trying to fight the bad dreams and images of him with someone else, while I lay in his bed with child.

Finally, one night, I stopped throwing up and could move around and eat what I wanted. I thought that something was wrong, but remembered that I had read in a book that the sickness would come to an end after the first or second trimester. I was happy, but then I started to really realize how alone I was, and that he was just not a part of my life. Devastated, I called him and told him that we needed to talk; I knew that this relationship was not going to last and that he didn't care. He called me back and said that he was going to come home so that we could talk. I assumed that because I was having his child that I was important to him, but I thought wrong, because he didn't show up until four hours later.

I turned to him and asked him why he treated me with such disrespect. I asked him to understand that he was all I had and that I was all he had, and we were having a baby. I reminded him of the conversation that we'd had that night at my sister's apartment, and asked if he remembered that he'd said that he would take care of me. I didn't understand and wanted him to explain. I wanted him to tell me if he wanted me to leave or if he wanted me to stay. I wanted to know if he really loved me like he said he did, or if he set out to get something, got it, and then wanted to quit it. I wanted to know if he wanted to be with me or if there was someone else. I wanted to know that I was the one for him and that I meant something to him, because he meant something to me.

He turned on the light; his face was swollen and he was sweating. I said to him, "What is going on? Are you ok?" He turned, and with a numb tongue and dripping coming from his nose, he said that he was addicted to cocaine. I said, "You're what!"

He said, "I am addicted to cocaine." I sat and looked at him and was at a loss for words. I couldn't believe it--the man that I was going to have a child by was addicted to drugs. For goodness sake, I was in Youth to Youth, the drug-free program when I was younger, and my mother always told me to stay away from drugs. Now look at me: I was with a crack head. I started to cry and didn't understand why this was happening. I turned and asked how long he had been addicted to cocaine, and how it started.

He explained that it was just about six months ago that he and a few of his friends were sitting around a table, playing cards and drinking. One of his boys pulled out a bag of cocaine and said that it was better than weed. They said that it would take you to another level, and that it would get you high instantly. He said that everyone decided to do this, including him, and they had all been hooked since. I turned and asked who they were, and wanted to know when he was going to stop. He said that he was cheating on me, but not with a girl--with the drug, and that he could not resist. I didn't know what I was going to do and didn't understand what he wanted me to say. I was scared for my child and thought that he or she would be addicted to drugs. I wanted to hit him. I hated him and loved him at the same time, and didn't understand why and how I would even get involved with a man of this nature.

He then turned and said that he needed my help. I thought to myself how I could help him; after all, I didn't know what to expect from him anymore. I asked him how I could help, and he said that I would need to be with him at all times, and so that's what I did. I became his right-hand girl, delivering and selling drugs with him, trying to understand how to weigh the drugs and how much profit it would turn over, holding the items on me when riding in the car, holding thousands of dollars at a time, and coming home to count it out for him.

As time progressed, he started to get more and more distant from me. I was starting to show and he was getting concerned about me running around with him. I knew that I was going to lose the battle of helping him, and didn't know if I should force myself on him or back off. Sometimes, I would not see him for days, and he spent more and more time away from home. I needed someone to talk to, and I only had one good male friend at the time. He was the one that I could always count on. He knew that I was a good person, and told me to hang in there and I would get though it. I told him that I was not sure if he loved me anymore. I told him about the drug problem and constant arguments. I told him that I was losing my mind and didn't know what to do anymore.

It was a messed-up beginning to life; I had a baby on the way, and was depending on him to take care of me with drug money; my man was addicted to drugs; I was always arguing with him, and didn't really have a place to call home. Yeah, love made me stay around; I wish that I could say that and believe it, but it was not the case. Love had nothing to do with it anymore. There was a whole new person that I was getting ready to birth and he or she needed a father. I didn't want him or her to grow up without one, as I had. The memory that I had of my father was everlasting, and I wanted my son or daughter to have the same chance as me when I was a child, up until my father passed. Now, I'm not making excuses; I thought deep down in my heart that this man wanted to be with me and that he cared.

I knew that he was addicted to drugs, drinks, and never comes home. I felt that when we were together and not arguing or fighting, he expressed his love for me and the child on the way. I was the queen of making scenarios in my mind, and I justified the behavior that was going on within my household.

Now, I was seven months pregnant, and my body was starting to break down. I couldn't carry my child any longer. My doctor decided to place me in the hospital for a period of time to make sure that I didn't experience premature labor. They wanted to make sure that the lungs were developed and strong. He stayed with me a few nights and then went on his way. I was released to go home about three weeks later, with restrictions. My doctor assigned a nurse to come and monitor me on a weekly basis to ensure that my child's heartbeat was regular. I was so depressed that he was never around. I cried everyday and trying to figure out what was wrong with me. I never could get it quite right. What did I do? Should I have done something different in bed? Should I have cooked different meals? Should I have been out messing around on him? Should I have dressed a certain way? What could it be that made this man not like me and want to be around me? I asked all the questions.

Then it dawned on me that it was not me that was the problem, and I needed to make a decision about what I was going to do when the baby was born. I proposed in my mind that I had to get out of this situation and find somewhere to live. The more and more he was gone, the angrier I became with him, thinking to myself that he was with someone else and that I was being disrespected. I could not contain myself any longer. I started to fight with him every time he walked in the door. I would pull at his clothes, scratch his face, and attack his body. I wanted him to feel everything that he was currently putting me through. He became my enemy and target. I dismissed the fact that I was expecting, and the health of myself and the baby; I was so fixated on him that nothing much counted anymore. Why was he doing this to me, and why did he turn me into this angry person? Why did he mistreat me like I was unimportant? Did he care about what I was going through, not only dealing with the challenges of him taking my pureness away from me, but stealing my peace?

My peace of mind

My peace of control

My peace of grace

My peace of independence

My peace of confidence

My peace of communication

My peace of love

My peace of self-respect

My peace of pride

My peace of kindness

He stole from me and I was left with nothing. It's hard to imagine someone taking that much away from you, isn't it? But, it happens to you. I believe that it can. It can happen to your brother, mother, father, sister, aunt, cousins, and friends. The truth is that many of us are going through what I just described, feeling sorry for ourselves and holding on to something that we should have released a long time ago. I'm not sure when I started to lose myself. I often wondered if it was when I had my first-base experience with a guy, or if it was with this man that I was pregnant by.

Daily, I took showers, trying to hide my tears and trying to wash away the pain, dirt, and the aggravation that I had caused myself. Self-inflicted pain is what I call it. I didn't plan to harm myself, but I was dying on the inside, wishing things would turn for the better and not continue on this downward spiral. I spent days lying in bed, wishing my life was different, and exchanging my thoughts of happiness with thoughts of death. I penalized myself for the choices that I had made, and the repercussions of those decisions. I felt raped of my innocence constantly. I was just plain lost.

It seems I was blaming most, if not all, of my situation on him. So what part did I play? I can honestly say that it was who I was and what I expected from this person that made our relationship what it was. I could not accept from the beginning of the relationship who he was. I didn't agree with him drinking, smoking, doing drugs, going to strip clubs, and hanging out all night with his friends. I didn't accept his appearance, language use, and problem-solving skills. I didn't accept his quiet comments and lack of attention. I didn't accept his lack of desire to become something more than a drug dealer and accept responsibility for all his actions. I didn't accept his lack of courage and motivation. I never could accept him. I wondered if he could see what I was trying to do. I wanted the family that I had when I was eight, the family that died with my father. I wanted someone to share my joy, someone to share my insight, and someone to talk to and hold on a quiet night while the children lay still in bed.

Could he see my vision? It was so clear to me, but not clear for him. Could he feel it all around me? "What should I do?" I asked myself, trying and trying to hang on for dear life. I was still trying to understand why this was happening. My life was never supposed to turn out like this. Suddenly, in the midst of all the emotions, I felt a trickle come down my leg.

You Saved My Life

My water broke and I was off to the hospital to have the baby. I didn't know what to expect or how much pain I was going to feel. I was not ready for what was in store for me. The nurse came into the room and sedated me, with the doctor following shortly after. The doctor asked if I would like to have an epidural, which was a numbing medication that was used to help suppress the pain of child birth. I said yes, and the doctor gave orders to the nurse. The nurse came in with a long needle and told me that she would have to stick this in my spine. I sat up in the bed and the nurse took the clothes off my back. She rubbed me with some sanitizing liquid. I then felt the worst pain of my life, or so I thought; there was a powerful pinch, and instantly, I started to have relief from the contractions.

The contractions were coming fast. My mother, sister, and the father of my daughter were in the room. For a few moments, the conversation went on as though I was not having a baby. The doctor was talking to my mother and my sister was talking to the nurse. The attention was not on me; and again, I felt that no one cared. The doctor turned and said that I was too relaxed. He decided to take down the medication so that I could feel the contractions coming, and I did. I started to push and push, and continued to push until 11:00 p.m. that night. My daughter was born at 11:05 p.m. When my child came out, she was blue. I thought that she was dead, and then I heard a cry. The doctor said that I had a baby girl, and she weighed four pounds and thirteen ounces. I only had a second to look at her. At first, I didn't know what to think or say. I knew that I had just had a baby, but the reality still didn't kick in. The nurse and the doctor took care of me, and then I went to another room. Usually, the baby would come in the room with you, but because my daughter was premature, they had her in a special room. The hospital called it the "nuke room." A day later, after my epidural wore off, the nurse suggested that I go into the room and see my baby girl. As I approached the room, I had to put on a sterile cap and gown to enter and hold her. She was very tiny, and I was not able to take her out of her bed.

The doctors had wires running in and out of her, as well as the feeding and oxygen tube. I didn't know what to do or say. The doctor said that she would have to be in the hospital for two weeks, or until she was able to eat.

Scared Little Black Girl

A few days later, I packed my bags and left the hospital without my baby.

I returned home, and the depression of the house kicked in and I felt the hurt of not having my baby with me. I looked around and found that I needed to do something better. I had to get my own place. After about a week of going to the hospital, I decided to go sign up to get Section Eight or low-income housing. My friend picked me up and took me to several places to make sure that I got it done. I also had to get rides to the hospital so that I could see my baby. It was almost time for her to come home. It had been two weeks, and the doctor called me to say that I could bring my baby home. They gave me special instructions to take care of her and instructions on feedings.

When I brought my daughter home, I knew that things were going to change between us. I believed that he would be home more and would want to be around his family. I thought wrong, because the situation got worse. Having a baby was no joke. I knew that I was in for challenging times. I was up all night and day with my child. My daughter had colic, which people refer to as a crying spell. I felt like it was a deaf spell to the parent. Up all night, she would cry, throw up, poop, cry, sleep, wake, and cry some more. The doctor said that there was nothing that I could do about it, and gave me some instructions to soothe her when she was crying.

I never got any sleep. He was never there to help me at night. He would hang out all night and then come home in the morning, if at all. One night, I was so tired and she was up all night crying. I went downstairs and found him lying on the couch, sleeping. I nudged him and asked him to take her. He said no, and that he was sleeping. I begged and pleaded with him. Finally, I went upstairs, got her rocker, and put her in it as she started to cry. I sat her beside him as she was still crying. I turned and began to walk up the steps.

He then turned and said, "Bitch!" I turned and attacked him with a slap. He jumped up, pushed me down, and began to kick me. His mom and sister heard the commotion and came running down the stairs. They pulled him off me, and I ran outside, crying. His mother joined me outside, and said that maybe it was time for me to go. She asked me if I could live with my mom or sister; I said no. Later that day, I called one of my friends and said that I was homeless, and asked if I could live with her for a few months. She said that I could, and I packed my bags. I called my mom to see if she could help me move. He left as I was packing all my things. I took everything that belonged to me: the bed, dresser, clothes, all the baby's items, and the food that I had bought.

Later, my sister called me and said that she knew a friend that was selling a car. The asking price for the car was five hundred dollars. My sister's friend accepted my offer of one hundred dollars and making payments. I started to look for a job, and several of my friends helped me by watching my daughter. I looked and found a job at a local truck-loading company. The company mainly consisted of men loading and unloading trucks. Not even six weeks after having my baby, I was doing heavy lifting and slinging boxes, trying to make a living. The fact of the matter was that I was out on my own and I had no one to depend on.

It was hard, and I was exhausted daily, staying up all night and going to work to do heavy lifting. I worked and worked, until I got my own place. My mom got an apartment for my cousin, and at the last minute, he said that he could not move in. She gave the apartment to me. Without surprise, by the time I moved in, my daughter's father and I were back together. So he packed his bags and I packed mine. We moved into our first apartment. I was so happy to have something that I could call my own; after all, I had been living with other people for a long time. I forgot how it felt. I thought to myself, this was going to be a change for him and me, and that things would be different living in a house without his family.

Things started off nice; he went to the store and got food, and he made it seem like we were a happy family. We would go out and have fun, and come home acting like we were married. The feelings I had for him were resurfacing, and I knew that we were going to make it. Then, before I could even say that I was happy and in love, he started to revert back to who he really was. I was left alone again, but this time, I had no child in me and no one around to observe everything that I did. I had a car and just a little money, enough for me to go out to the clubs and hang out with my friends. And that's what I did.

It was payback in my mind; he did not come home and neither did I. My daughter was taken care of and I had a set babysitter that adored her, so I didn't worry. He started to go out of town and leave me notes, treating me like some roommate. The more and more we were apart, the faster I fell out of love with him, and could not stand being around him. His friends became his family, and I was some person that he would have sex with when he had the time. Bitter, I started to talk to other guys, and go out to the movies and on dates. If I had plans and knew that it was a possibility for him to come home, I would call him and argue, just so he would stay away from the house. At times, I would have other guys come over and watch a movie or sit outside talking, feeling guiltless about my actions.

In my heart, I knew that it was time for me to leave him, but because of our child, I felt it necessary for me to stay. I understood the things that I was doing, playing this hurtful game with myself, child, and him, but didn't know what else I could do. Please understand that this was my first for everything, and I thought that he had the answers that were right for me. Just around six months later, he came home and I was sick. He asked me what was wrong, and I told him that I was pregnant.

He sat down and said that he wanted me to keep the baby. I looked at him and time froze. I remembered those words before and knew that I would have to make the best choice for me. I didn't understand how he could have those same words come out of his mouth; he was never there to help me with the child that we already had. I didn't know what to do, and was going to make sure that I did what was best for me this time. I thought about it for a while, and understood that if I was going to do this, I would be in this alone.

A few weeks later, still lying around and trying to make the best choice, I came home and there was a note on the table, saying that he was leaving and going on a trip with his friends to Atlanta. While I was at home, sick and with a baby on my hip, he was traveling and enjoying life. After all, this was not the first time that he had left me and I didn't know where he was going. He was out having fun, while I was at home, trying to figure out how to be a mom and live-in girlfriend at the same time.

I decided that I was not going to proceed with having the child. When he returned from the trip, I had already called and spoken with the abortion clinic to schedule an appointment. The cost of the abortion was a little over three hundred dollars, and I told him that he needed to give me half of the money. He was completely against it, but said that he would support me in whatever I needed to do. I told him that I was not going back on my decision.

The day of the appointment came, and he came along with me and my mother. The nurse called me to have me fill out some paperwork, and what seemed to be such a simple decision at that time would haunt me the rest of my life. The nurse directed me to take a pregnancy test to ensure that indeed I was pregnant, and the results came back as I had speculated; I was expecting. I asked the nurse what the next step was. She informed me that I would have to make a payment, and sent me into an office that looked to be used at one point as a janitorial supply closet. The lady that sat behind the desk had hardness to her attitude, and it almost seemed as if I was disturbing her. She asked me a series of questions about my medical insurance, reviewed the procedure with me, and explained all the forms that I was completing. She advised me that there were two different procedures; because of the money, I decided to stay awake during the surgery. After the questioning, the staff instructed me to review a movie that consisted of terminating a baby. The movie said that I was a murderer, but not in those words. The review of the movie explained how many weeks I had been pregnant and what development stage I was in at that very moment. I sat and contemplated my choices; I had memories of being mistreated and abused, disliked, hated, immature, and not ready for any additional responsibility. Once the video was over, I was instructed to return to the lobby and make another appointment to go back before the next procedure.

Riding in the car, I reviewed the information the nurse had given me and the information showed me pictures of what was going to happen to my unborn child. I felt bad and was unsure at that moment what choice was the best; after all, at this stage in my pregnancy, my child had ears, hands, feet, and was developing daily. I knew that it wasn't the right thing to do, but I knew that I could not afford to take care of another child. When I came home that night, I looked around and wondered how I had taken care of myself for so long. My apartment was empty with just a television and couch, I had no dining table, and I slept on an air mattress that deflated. Although my daughter had all the things that she needed, I knew how much of a battle it was for me to take care of her, and with her father and I arguing all the time, I knew that I would not survive another pregnancy with him or he would kill me. Before I knew it, the day of the second appointment arrived. The doctors had to do a surgical procedure, due to the number of weeks that I had been pregnant, which would cause me to dilate. The first step started with an ultrasound. The nurse called my name and told me to enter the room. She told me that I would need to take off all my clothes and sit on the table. The doctor came in about fifteen minutes later and introduced himself to me. I gasped for a breath of air and introduced myself to him. He started to speak to me about the procedure and wanted to make sure that I was certain about the choices that I was making. He assured me that everything was going to be okay and instructed me to lie on the table. I lay down, frightened, on the hard cold table and placed my feet in the stirrups. He said that he was going to do an ultrasound first, as he placed the jelly on my stomach. I understood that this time was real and that there was no turning back. I proceeded to ask him if everything looked okay, and he replied yes. As he was looking at the ultrasound machine, my mother entered the room. She stood beside him and he pointed to an image on the monitor. He told my mom to take a look at my twins. I felt a sudden urge to stop him from doing anything else, but by the time I realized what he had said to my mother, it was too late. The medication had already been inserted in my uterus. I said I wanted to think about it, and he told me that it was too late. He walked up to the table, placed his hand on my shoulder, and told me I had made the right decision. Disgusted, I started to cry; all of a sudden, I was alone again with a feeling of failure and a bundle of choices that were wrong.

I went home that night and prepared myself for the next day, and as usual, this so-called man that loved me so much dropped me off and left to run the streets. I never felt better about the choice that I was making not to have any other children with him. There was no turning back at this point, so I accepted what I was doing, and justified the reason that I was making the decision based on what he was doing to me everyday. Morning arrived and I had to be there bright and early. He went with me; on the way to the clinic, the car ride was silent and there was worry and hate in the air. As we pulled into the parking lot, there were people who were standing outside, calling me a murderer. I never felt so dirty and as I walked in the building; the looks of rage on their faces were unforgettable. They chanted words from the bible and said that I was going to hell. I came to the front door, which was locked; I rang the bell and someone came to the door to make sure that I was indeed a patient.

I walked into the waiting room, and to my surprise, there were about ten other women that looked just as scared as me. The faces of young, old, white, and black women were all around me. We shared a common emotion of fear and regret. The nurse called my name and said that the doctor was ready for me. I walked into the old room and was told to take off my clothes. The nurse checked my vital signs and inserted an IV in my arm. She told me that it would be a quick procedure, painless, but I would feel some pressure. As the nurse left the room, I still had no idea about what I was going to encounter. The doctor came in and asked me to relax; I tried. He proceeded to have me lay on the table and told me to put my legs in the stirrups; I did. Immediately following, I heard him turn on what sounded like a vacuum. All of a sudden, I felt a tremendous amount of pain. This pain was like no other; it was the pain of life being sucked out of my body. I never knew the hurt of hearing the bones of my unborn children crushed as I glanced to the side of the table; I saw the blood and bones being passed through a tube. I felt the breath come out of me at that very moment. I never felt so disconnected from myself, and felt as if I was committing murder; I screamed out in pain and disgust.

The doctor stood up and said that he was done, as if he had just preformed some type of miracle. He told me again that I was making the best choice. He told me that I was young, and that I had my whole life ahead of me. I never understood why that doctor kept telling me that; maybe it was because I was his patient. Maybe he saw the sadness in my eyes, or maybe he saw something in me that I couldn't see in myself. Whatever the case, I knew that didn't want to go through the same thing again. Waiting in the lobby, I looked at the father of my daughter and the children that I had just murdered with disgust, thinking, if you were only a man and could take care of your family, I would have never done this. I'd blamed it all on him and his shortcomings. I could not understand why he could not feel my pain, frustration, and bitterness towards him. Nonetheless, the thing that amazed me was that as he looked at me, I saw him giving me the same looks, and he had the exact feeling that I had at that point. He didn't understand why I did this to him and the family that he so wanted. He did not understand why I hated him so, and stayed with him. He didn't understand why I didn't respect his decision to keep the babies, and why I was doing this to him.

And It Was Worse

After the surgery, I never felt the same about him again. I wish I could say that I was never a murderer again, but I can't. This abortion thing became my method of birth control. While the first was painful, with time, my soul became cold, and I committed murder time and time again. Acts of being lazy, and unwillingness to protect myself against his self-gratification were all too common. It made little difference to me if we had protection or not, because I just didn't care anymore, and it showed. I used to ask myself why I continued to live this life of deception, and my discarded babies would come to me in my dreams. Their faces and voices would hunt me for years and years to come. I knew that I had to end this pattern of birth control. It seemed that every year I would have the procedure done, and after the third one, my body was cold and numb from the decisions that I had made. I started to encounter the side effects from having the procedure completed time and time again. My body ached at night, and I had tremendous pain in my abdomen, which sometimes brought me to my knees from the contracting pain. The inside of my body was weak.

But did he know or did he care about this pain that I was going through? I think that he cared in his own selfish way. I never understood how he felt about me, us, and the family that we had created. The whole relationship was made under false pretenses, and I never would have guessed that we would end up separated. After about three years of all the mess, I gave up on him and the way we were living. I couldn't take the drugs, arguing, and constant worries about other people and their perception of us. I'm sure he made me out to be this overly jealous monster, and I made him out to be a monster as well. I never appreciated him and he never appreciated me. I never knew who he was and he never knew who I was.

Let's face it: we were young and involved in something that was bigger than the both of us. We played house and did a great job at first, and I was a little girl that had to grow up quickly, missing some of the most important years of my life. I have to agree with the saying that women develop faster than men; it is true in some cases. I think that we are wiser in some aspects, but not in all. In my opinion, he knew that he was over his head in responsibility and so did I. I decided to fight, in an attempt to make it. He decided to try to make it disappear in his mind and surroundings. I never knew that he was in captivity within his own mind, body, and soul. I always thought it was the things that I was doing, when in the end, it was not me and not him, but the level of maturity that was the root of the problem, and the acceptance of responsibility.

On a cold and lonely night when the pain had surfaced and the loneliness was unbearable, I made a decision to change my life at that time, and wondered how a life would be with someone who loved and enjoyed spending time with me. I knew life was never going to be perfect, because of the lessons that I had already learned and the trust issues that were already created. No one can understand the pain that a person endures during the trials of their lives. We look at people and think that, because they are well put together, life has treated them well and they have accomplished life goals. The reality of that is slim; to find a perfect person is impossible, and the ability to accept someone for who they are and what they will become is left up to the individual person.

The decision I made was a hard choice, but I chose to make sure that my daughter could see a brighter day, a day when she would see her mother out of pain and enjoying what was created for us here on earth; a day that she could read and know that people are not perfect, and that although many are told they will be nothing, they can become something; a day where she would feel defeated because of a heartbreak or a choice that she made, and know that it's okay, because I can be her example of what not to do. I chose to have a better life, and no one could take that way. The dreams I had were mine; the confidence

I had was mine; and the peace that came over my heart and mind was finally there when I decided to leave.

I thought about my mother and how she worked hard all her life to give us the things that we needed, and even though for that last year of high school my mother was gone, I still had the values that she planted in me as a child. I knew that this was not supposed to be my life. I was supposed to go to college, live that American dream, and do great things in life, but life took a turn and I went with it. Do I regret what happened to me? I wish I could say that I did, but I don't. My experiences are those of many untold stories: the women who are beaten everyday by boyfriends, husbands, and fathers; the children that are left alone on cold nights, wishing their parents would come home and give them the attention they have been seeking; the men who want to do the right thing and support their families, but can't see past circumstances; the emotional outburst of lonely nights, depressed environments, and hopeless situations. I understand that these are the ways of the world, and although my life story will go on beyond this book and the experience of life will continue to grow in me and around me everyday, I know now that we all have choices to make; no one can make choices for us. I decided to live and come out of the shell that someone placed me in. It is now that I understand that people are in captivity within their own surroundings. I challenge you to ask yourself.

Scared Little Black Girl

No Need to Hide

I ask, have I come out of hiding?
Have we learned from our life lessons?
Have we created a pattern?
Have we suppressed our feelings?
Have we passed on our pain?
Have we set an example?
Have we wondered what people see when they look at us?
Have we tried to change or save someone?
Have we put ourselves on the right track?
Have we turned our heads and seen our futures?
Are we in isolation?
Have we decided what our agendas are going to be?
Have we put ourselves to the test?
Have we put our lives on the line?
Have we faced the reality that people are not going to love us the way that we love them?
Have we placed value in ourselves?
Have we accomplished our goals?
Have we gone over and beyond our steps?
Have we pleased someone else and forgotten about ourselves?
And when someone comes up to you and asks who you are, will you know the truth?

Printed in the United States
133415LV00001B/18/A